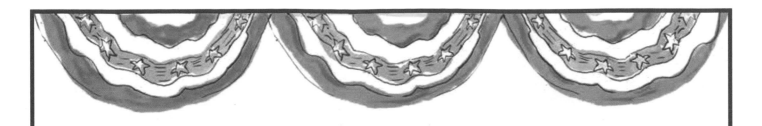

Have You Heard About Lady Bird?

★ ★ ★ ★ ★

POEMS ABOUT OUR FIRST LADIES

–BY–

MARILYN SINGER ★ NANCY CARPENTER

–ILLUSTRATED BY–

𝒟ISNEY • HYPERION

Los Angeles   New York

To two ladies who are first in my book, Rotem Moscovich and Dina Sherman —M.S.

To my dear friend, Carolyn, and the #MeToo movement —N.C.

ACKNOWLEDGMENTS

Thanks to Steve Aronson, Brenda Bowen, Joann Hill, Heather Crowley, Becky Dalzell, and all the good folks at Hyperion who made this book possible. —M.S.

Text copyright © 2018 by Marilyn Singer
Illustrations copyright © 2018 by Nancy Carpenter

First Edition, October 2018
10 9 8 7 6 5 4 3 2 1
FAC-029191-18243
Printed in Malaysia

This book was set in 16-point Cloister/Fontspring
Designed by Trish Parcell

Library of Congress Cataloging-in-Publication Data

Names: Singer, Marilyn, author • Carpenter, Nancy, illustrator.
Title: Have you heard about lady bird? : poems about our first ladies / by
Marilyn Singer ; illustrations by Nancy Carpenter.
Description: First Edition. • Los Angeles ; New York : Disney HYPERION, 2018.
Identifiers: LCCN 2016019313 • ISBN 9781484726600 (hardcover) • ISBN 148472660X (hardcover)
Classification: LCC PS3569.I546 A6 2018 • DDC 811/.54—dc23
LC record available at https://lccn.loc.gov/2016019313

Reinforced binding
Visit www.DisneyBooks.com

FIRST LADIES

We know Eleanor Roosevelt, Abigail Adams,
    but what about those other madams—
the many First Ladies of our nation
    who held that most demanding station
        from our country's uncertain conception
          right up to the present day.
Those women who knew how to host a reception,
    how much or how little to say.
The ones who welcomed public life,
    or chose to hide away.
Who fought for causes on their own,
    or preferred to stay behind the throne.
How many have we read about or even recall?
Julia Tyler? Florence Harding?
    It's time to meet them all.

MARTHA DANDRIDGE CUSTIS WASHINGTON

(1789–1797)

Raised to be a planter's wife,
    taught how one behaves
as mistress of the household
    and the household slaves.
Widowed early, widowed wealthy,
    ran her own plantation,
met a fine young gentleman
    equal to her station.
Planned to have a peaceful life,
    with her new husband, George.
Then came the Revolution,
    that time at Valley Forge,
those visits to the other camps
    where winters were not pretty.
And later, the election,
    with that move to New York City,
the country's acting capital
    she likened to a jail.
Though this was not the life she chose,
    she did not choose to fail.
"Lady Presidentess," dear wife of our first leader,
    did not bemoan, she set the tone,
        for all who would succeed her.

ABIGAIL SMITH ADAMS

(1797–1801)

In careful hand "My dearest friend"
    began the letters she would send
to her husband, John,
to help them carry on
throughout their many years apart—
    of political opinions, tales of the heart,
    struggles with their home and farm,
    keeping their children safe from harm.
She wrote about her lonely nights,
    and the need for women's rights,
    how men would be tyrants if they could.
She struggled for our country's good.
When John became the president,
    she deemed her sacrifice well spent.

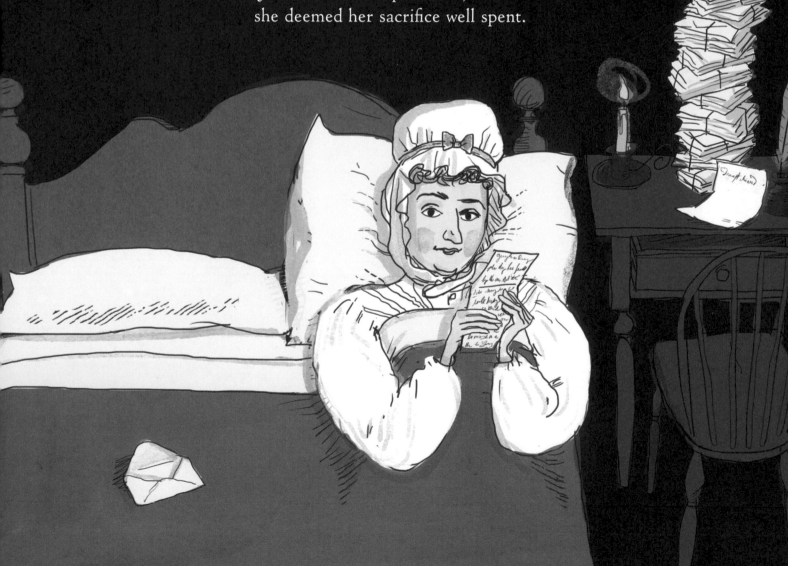

MARTHA WAYLES SKELTON JEFFERSON

(d. 1782)

A sprightly hostess at Monticello,
    she played pianoforte to his violin.
But their music never echoed through the White House.
    Her role was taken by her next of kin.
Do not remarry when I'm gone, ailing Martha bid.
Thomas vowed he never would—and he never did.

DOLLEY PAYNE TODD MADISON
(1809–1817)

It was not folly
that made Dolley declare
she'd not be leaving without retrieving
that portrait of Washington,
symbol of independence.
She had to protect it from British vengeance
before the soldiers burned down
her house and the town.
This beloved First Lady then grew in esteem
for more than her parties and delicious ice cream.

ELIZABETH KORTRIGHT MONROE

(1817–1825)

Her looks, her style caused quite a stir.
She loved the French, and they loved her.
But times in France had grown quite sinister,
  when James Monroe was foreign minister.
Aristocrats were under threat,
  including their friend, Lafayette,
and his wife—imprisoned, slated
  soon to be decapitated.
Elizabeth chose to intervene
  and save her from the guillotine.
The French, with fondness, dubbed her then
  their "beautiful American."
But as First Lady of our land,
  she sometimes seemed a bit *too* grand.
She lacked the democratic touch.
Yankees didn't like her much.

LOUISA CATHERINE JOHNSON ADAMS

(1825–1829)

It's clear she was a prodigy,
who played the harp, wrote poetry.
She hoped there'd be equality—
    she wanted to be heard.

Her husband was dismissive
(at times perhaps derisive):
Women ought to be submissive.
    He didn't listen to a word.

Through losses, grief, and much turmoil,
through many years on foreign soil,
she was faithful, she was loyal—
    a diplomatic wife.

She faced dangers every day,
crossing Europe in a sleigh,
rode through fields where soldiers lay.
    She almost lost her life.

When he got to lead the nation,
did he show his admiration,
offer thanks, appreciation
    that she'd helped fulfill his dream?

No.

But later on when their ambition
was to fight for abolition,
they worked jointly for their mission.
    Then at last John held Louisa in esteem.

And the Adamses were finally a team.

RACHEL DONELSON ROBARDS JACKSON

(d. 1828)

Divorce.
The source of many a scandal.
It was difficult for her to handle
how society chose to disparage
     her happy second marriage,
how the anti-Jackson journals out for blood
     were always slinging mud.
Publicity was a curse.
Things might have gotten worse
     after his inauguration.
But she didn't join the celebration.
She died and was buried in her new party dress.
Death can stop the breath
     of the most malicious press.

HANNAH HOES VAN BUREN

(d. 1819)

Pious, sweet, and charitable? Perhaps. Who really knows
     much about Van Buren's wife, once known as Hannah Hoes?
In Albany, she caught TB and died in dreadful stages.
How often was she spoken of in those 800 pages
     he wrote about his life and work—a ponderous endeavor—
of days when she was by his side? The simple answer: never.

ANNA TUTHILL SYMMES HARRISON

(1841)

She wasn't the least bit hesitant.
She didn't want him to be president.
War hero, congressman, now gladly retired,
William was popular, seasoned, admired.
They pressed him to run—he had the Whigs' backing.
Soon after he won, she found herself packing
for her trip to D.C. to be at his side.
But it was too late. Her husband had died.
The Congress agreed (perhaps with dissension)
to give her a sizable First Widow's pension.

She lived another score of years, was dignified in grief—
the only First Lady whose grandson
was also Commander in Chief.

LETITIA CHRISTIAN TYLER

(1841–1842)

JULIA GARDINER TYLER

(1844–1845)

Upstairs in a wheelchair, John Tyler's first wife,
 Letitia, was rarely seen.
In contrast, his second, the spirited Julia,
 chose to hold court like a queen.
Born in Virginia, Letitia, demure,
 was wise about shutting her mouth.
Outspoken Julia, a native New Yorker,
 took up defense of the South.
When the war ended, the Confederates paid
 for their rebel affiliation.
But Julia, with verve and a whole lot of nerve,
 didn't suffer humiliation.

She eagerly offered her bio to the *first* First Ladies compiler.
Maintaining her fame, she flaunted the name:
 "Mrs. Ex-President Tyler."

SARAH WHITSETT CHILDRESS POLK

(1845–1849)

Uninterested in domesticity,
she preferred discussing policy—
from using new technology
to achieving Manifest Destiny
(that is, extending westerly—
our God-given duty, to be specific,
to expand this land to the Pacific).
With commitment and persistence,
she advised and gave assistance.

But the fight for equal rights wasn't part of her plan.
She believed a woman's place was *behind* her leading man.

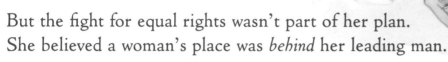

MARGARET "PEGGY" MACKALL SMITH TAYLOR

(1849–1850)

Yes, I chose to marry a soldier.
Wherever we wandered, I held our fort steady.
How was I to know he'd become a legend,
    America's own "Old Rough and Ready"?

When he fought so bravely in the Mexican War
I prayed God would grant him protection.
When they nominated him to be president,
    I prayed that he'd lose the election.

ABIGAIL POWERS FILLMORE

(1850–1853)

My father was a preacher. He did not fare well in matters pecuniary.
I became a teacher, with help from the books in his large and impressive library.

One of my students was yearning to learn. It was obvious he had the skill for
getting ahead and getting along—that diligent young Millard Fillmore.

By the time we were wed, he had taken up law. His practice had started to grow.
We established a college and a library, too, in the city of Buffalo.

He soon entered Congress, became the V.P. He wished me to be by his side.
But then came a shock that we couldn't foresee—President Taylor had died.

We moved to the White House, resplendent with rooms: offices, parlors, and nooks.
But I was appalled—in *not one* was installed a goodly collection of books.

For one of the spaces, I ordered bookcases. It became a delightful retreat.
I would have spent many more hours up there had Millard not suffered defeat.

But we weren't sorry to exit the White House. We were sorely in need of a rest.
A difficult quest to govern this country—I wished those poor Pierces the best.

JANE MEANS APPLETON PIERCE

(1853–1857)

He promised no more politics.
But ambition is a devil.
Another might revel
      in her husband's nomination,
but for me the honor was tainted.
When he gave me the news, I fainted.
Lord, let me live in mourning.
I did not heed God's warning.
Two sons already lost
and then our dearest third was fated
      to die before the inauguration.
I did not choose this life—being a president's wife.

HARRIET "HAL" REBECCA LANE (JOHNSTON)

(1857–1861)

I think Uncle James always liked my spunk.
I in turn loved my guardian, Nunc.
With no wife, he needed my social graces—
seating guests in appropriate places.
Politics is an agreeable game
for those who have the mind and heart.
But more than politics, I love art.
I told Nunc that there ought to be
a first-rate national gallery.
Somewhere to leave works I will have collected.
Someplace I know they will be well respected,
where people will view them with pleasure for free.
I'd like that as my legacy.

MARY ANNE TODD LINCOLN

(1861–1865)

Yankee journalist:	She's a spy for the South.
Rebel journalist:	She's a traitor to the Cause.
Union soldier:	She's a merciful nurse.
Her dressmaker:	She's a good soul—with flaws.
Northern housewife:	Buys those dresses and china, throws extravagant banquets.
Mr. Lincoln:	Flub-dubs for the White House while our soldiers have no blankets.
Southern housewife:	She eats cake while we sorely need bread.
Both housewives:	I hear tell that she's touched in the head! Holding séances, shouting shrilly.
Her dressmaker:	She's grieving for her dear son, Willie. She thinks a First Lady should look refined— and that all slaves should be free. She always speaks her mind.
Journalists:	Of all the first ladies, she is the worst!
Her dressmaker:	She's an unlucky woman—kindly and cursed.

ELIZA McCARDLE JOHNSON

(1865–1869)

They had such similar roots.
She understood making sandals.
He understood sewing suits.

They treasured their Tennessee.
But she favored abolition.
He was fine with slavery.

She taught him to be a good speaker,
to enter and win debates,
befitting an office seeker.

With politics his profession,
he rose to be chosen V.P.,
by standing against secession.

She planned to remain in their state—
her illness was taking its toll.
It wasn't to be her fate.

In April, a great tragedy.
He was suddenly president.
She joined him in dismal D.C.

He soon fell out of favor—
insulted Congress, was impeached.
But her firmness didn't waver.

Adviser, assistant, his dear invalid,
she believed in her Andrew when few others did.

JULIA BOGGS DENT GRANT

(1869–1877)

The White House was
    the right house for Julia Dent Grant.
She loved being hostess,
    the toast of the town,
throwing a lavish party,
wearing a ravishing gown.
It was hard to conceive
    she'd ever have to leave
but Ulysses stood firm:
    there'd be no third term.
Came the next election,
    with the vote contested
Julia suggested they stick around.
But Congress soon made its decision—
    there'd be no more delays.
It was the last night
    in the White House for Julia Dent Grant.
She wept as she left it
    to Lucy Webb Hayes.

LUCY WARE WEBB HAYES

(1877–1881)

Believed in temperance, but not prohibition.
In women's education, but not their right to vote.
In setting an example—but not taking a position
    on controversial causes too risky to promote.

Concerned about Rutherford's reputation,
she considered each issue quite carefully.
Her husband acknowledged with much admiration:
She might not sway Congress, but oh, her influence on me!

21

LUCRETIA "CRETE" RUDOLPH GARFIELD

(1881)

Though a teacher, scholar, artist,
perhaps one of the smartest
    first ladies,
Lucretia (known as Crete)
shy, aloof, discreet,
    never quick to show emotion,
became known for her devotion.
Barely mended from malaria, still fatigued and frail,
she made haste by special rail on a desperate ride
    to her wounded husband's side.
The nation praised her stamina as James Garfield's nurse—
and, then, her quiet dignity following his hearse.

ELLEN "NELL" LEWIS HERNDON ARTHUR

(d. 1880)

While the nation mourned its fallen leader,
the new president mourned the love of his life,
his departed wife:
      beloved Nell,
          with whom he shared golden fleeting hours
             and soft, moonlit nights;
      beloved Nell,
          whose rich voice, now stilled,
             once reached exquisite heights.
He laid flowers at her portrait,
      gazed daily at her face,
             refused to let another take her place.
Though his sister served as hostess, a role she managed well,
      his only true First Lady was his beloved Nell.

FRANCES CLARA FOLSOM CLEVELAND (PRESTON)

(1886–1889)

Frances: He gave me my first baby carriage.
           And now he's won my hand in marriage.
           Yes, he is much older, but our ages don't matter.
           Gossip's merely gossip. Chatter's simply chatter.

Reporters: What is she doing?
             What is she saying?
             What is she wearing?
             Where is she staying?
             She sells papers, does our Frankie
             (though that nickname makes her cranky).

Frances: Such adoration! Such botheration! I suppose I'll let it pass.
           In order to help women of the working class,
           I'll host socials for shop girls, nurses, and maids,
           government clerks, women in the trades.
           I'll wield my fame as a positive force.

Tradesmen: We'll publish her picture to endorse
             pianos, perfumes, playing cards, pills.
             Her face is so iconic, you will want to buy this tonic.
             Mrs. Cleveland's sure to rid you of your ills.

Frances: These ridiculous endorsements! I did not give my consent.
           These rumors and these stories! What else will they invent?
           These trinkets and these knickknacks, all these souvenirs.
           It drives me mad, but I'll be glad to come back here in four more years.

CAROLINE LAVINIA SCOTT HARRISON

(1889–1892)

Next to such beauty, any woman would fade.
Next to such youth, I must have seemed staid.

I wanted to fix up the White House,
      to make it more majestic.
But then the papers claimed
      that I was too domestic.

I liked to dance, play music, paint—
      true passions, not frivolity.
I didn't protest in the streets,
      yet stood up for equality,

leading the Daughters of the American Revolution,
explaining how women could make a contribution.

I did what I could. I did what I should.
      I was clear about what I believed in.
Yet I was eclipsed then and now
      by Mrs. Grover Cleveland.

IDA SAXTON McKINLEY

(1897–1901)

Ida McKinley was not well.
She wasn't well at all.
Her poor head often ached.
And sometimes she would fall
      down in a faint or stare off into space.
William used a handkerchief
      to drape her blank-eyed face.
The medicines she took to deaden
      her pain left her listless and leaden.
A woman who'd once been independent,
      whose husband was now her chief attendant.
Yet she rallied to make the expedition
      to the Pan-American Exposition.
There, in a tragic twist of fate,
      her "Major," her beloved mate,
          was shot.
Then Ida did what most thought she could not:
      she stayed upright, unflagging, close by his side,
      clear-eyed and caring, six days till he died.

EDITH KERMIT CAROW ROOSEVELT

(1901–1909)

HELEN "NELLIE" LOUISE HERRON TAFT

(1909–1913)

Edith: I was content in the governor's mansion
        but Fate chose a new destination.
        Now we'll fix up the East Wing and add a new West Wing.
        The White House will have renovation!

Nellie: I went to the White House when I was sixteen.
         Mr. Rutherford Hayes was our president.
         That's when I determined that one of these days
         the place would have *me* as a resident.

Edith:	Six children to manage, a great many pets.
	Counselling behind the scenes.
Nellie:	I said, "Will, take the president's offer
	to supervise the Philippines!"
Edith:	I require my own social secretary
	with whom I have rapport.
Nellie:	How Will's career's advancing!
	He's now secretary of war!
Edith:	T.R. vows he will serve just one term,
	then pick someone to take his place....
Nellie:	Whomever he chooses is certain to win
	the next presidential race.
Edith:	T.R. has tapped Taft to succeed him.
	If he'd asked me, I would have said "No."
Nellie:	Though people may say I'm too pushy,
	I push Will where he most wants to go.
Edith:	It's over. The country's decided
	that William H. Taft is their man.
Nellie:	I'm going to dress up this city
	with cherry trees straight from Japan!

. . .

Edith:	Now T.R. thinks Taft's done a bad job,
	so he's formed a third party. He'll run.
Nellie:	T.R. has betrayed us and look where it got him....
Edith:	That Democrat Wilson has won.
Nellie:	Well, Will, you can now be chief justice.
	Our time in the White House is done.

ELLEN LOUISE AXSON WILSON

(1913–1914)

She loved roses,
    so delicate, so lush.
She captured them
    with oils and brush.
The teachers praised her splendid work.
    A fine career was surely in store.
But she put such dreams aside
    when she became his bride.
She loved painting,
    but she loved her Woodrow more.

EDITH BOLLING GALT WILSON

(1915–1921)

Some said she loved her Woodrow
    more than she did her country.
When he was broken by a stroke,
she decided to deceive the nation
about his incapacitation,
pretending he was fit to lead,
refusing to let him resign,
deciding what visitors he should see,
what papers to read or sign.
Some claimed a conspiracy,
some said a misdeed.
Some knew she did it for the love of Woodrow—
    with them, Edith Wilson agreed.

FLORENCE MABEL KLING HARDING

(1921–1923)

She had a head for business.
It was bound to take her far—
    ran a store, then a paper
    called the *Marion Daily Star*.
She had a nose for politics.
She was destined for success—
    was good at public speaking
    and at handling the press.
She had an ear for music,
and an eye for photo ops.
    She loved the moving pictures,
    thought Hollywood was tops!
She had a heart for women.
She knew they were a force.
    She'd encourage them to vote,
    tell them whom they should endorse.
She had a taste for matters
    both domestic and foreign.
Might she have done a better job
    than less ambitious Warren?

GRACE ANNA GOODHUE COOLIDGE

(1923–1929)

She had a perpetual smile.
    The French honored her for her style.
She'd be there on opening day
    each spring when the Red Sox would play.
Although she kept up with the news,
    she did not voice political views.
But at dinners where Calvin was terse,
    it was always her job to converse.
At the great loss of one of her boys,
    she grieved deeply, but still kept her poise.
Yet through everything she had to face,
    Grace Coolidge was renowned for her grace.

LOU HENRY HOOVER

(1929–1933)

She was not Louise, but Lou.
A tomboy whose favorite wish
      was to camp outdoors,
      to hunt and fish,
      who made no apology
      for studying geology—
      something few women would do.
She was Lou. She was not Louise.
She traveled to troubled places,
      learned to speak Chinese,
      helped many refugees.
She understood volunteering,
      giving to charity,
      but not government assistance
      or personal austerity.
Came the Depression,
      she made a bad impression,
      with frequent escapes to their country retreat,
      with the lavish parties she threw
      (though paid for by Bert and Lou).
Insulated by their wealth,
      she didn't have a clue
      why the public was so angry,
      why they kicked up so much dirt.
Relentlessly attacked,
Herbert Hoover soon was sacked.
And Lou (no, not Louise) left the White House
      deeply hurt.

ANNA ELEANOR ROOSEVELT
(1933–1945)

A chance to be First Lady?
Her first thought was, *Oh, no!*

She was on the board of unions,
  she was on the radio.
She fought for public housing, women's rights,
  world peace.
She worried, how she worried
  that her power would decrease—
she would lose her identity,
  become a nonentity,
spend her time in the White House checking for dust.
Eleanor Roosevelt was afraid that she would rust.

But instead, it wasn't so!
She could do more than ever:
  writing columns, giving speeches,
  preaching FDR's New Deal,
  taking on racism.
She did it all with zeal!

Controversial.
Influential.
Truly consequential.
Whether hated or adored,
she couldn't be ignored
  nor put upon a shelf.
A woman, a First Lady, in a class
  by herself.

WIPE OUT
RACIAL

ELIZABETH "BESS" VIRGINIA WALLACE TRUMAN

(1945–1953)

Not for her, touring coal mines,
holding conferences for the press,
visiting troops,
inspecting factories—
that was Eleanor, not Bess.
Yet nevertheless,
without her opinions,
he'd have been at a loss—
or so Harry said, for he called her "The Boss."

MAMIE GENEVA DOUD EISENHOWER

(1953–1961)

When Mamie Doud agreed to marry,
    did she know she'd wed the military?
What comforts did she miss the most,
    traveling from post to post,
    dealing with miserable places to stay,
    difficult weather, inadequate pay?
But she believed in their romance—
    and she had talent for finance,
    for management and entertaining.
The army gave her quite a training,
    prepared her for life in Washington, D.C.
Becoming First Lady suited her to a tee.

From homemaking, decorating,
    and choosing the guests who were invited to dine,
she felt, *Running the office is his job,*
    but running the White House is mine.

JACQUELINE LEE BOUVIER KENNEDY (ONASSIS)

(1961–1963)

We watched her on TV.
Elegant, glamorous,
in high fashion, in high places,
giving a White House tour.
Few could resist her allure.
We watched her on TV.
Championing the arts
and historical preservation.
Speaking with reserve,
but without reservation.
We heard her converse in foreign tongues,
We saw how she'd entrance
leaders of Russia, Pakistan, France.
We watched her on TV
at the funeral procession.
With her children at her side,
she was regal, dignified.
Mourning so much promise that could never be kept,
we watched her on TV.
We wept.

CLAUDIA ALTA "LADY BIRD" TAYLOR JOHNSON

(1963–1969)

"Lady Bird," her nanny called her,
    and it stuck.
"Bird," her husband called her,
    and it fit.
She loved things that flew.
She loved things that grew:
    bluebonnets instead of billboards,
    jonquils replacing junkyards.
She wanted blossoms everywhere,
clean water, clean air,
    things to heal the heart,
    lift the spirit,
    unravel adversity,
    drive away gloom.
She wanted to see the country
    bloom.

THELMA CATHERINE "PAT" RYAN NIXON

(1969–1974)

She endured:
planting cabbage, picking corn, doing household chores,
working as a janitor—sweeping many floors.
Taking every kind of job while getting a degree,
later teaching kids to type and do stenography.
Marrying a driven man accused of dirty tricks,
staying loyal, supportive though she hated politics.
Facing down their critics with mandatory smiles,
trekking to dangerous places, traveling thousands of miles.
Contending with detractors who'd constantly insult her,
living with a husband who chose not to consult her.
Dealing with a scandal and then his resignation,
exiting the White House in deep humiliation.

A once well-liked First Lady, her prestige now obscured,
she went home to California, and in private, she endured.

ELIZABETH "BETTY" ANN BLOOMER WARREN FORD

(1974–1977)

The word for her was "candid."
Betty Ford demanded
    that she wouldn't be branded
    a president's wife with no ideas of her own.
A modern dancer, she was bold.
When she had cancer, Betty Ford told
    the world. She broke the mold.
She let herself be known—
    from her views on women's rights
    to her struggles with addiction.
Betty Ford was always
    a woman of conviction.

ELEANOR ROSALYNN SMITH CARTER

(1977–1981)

They said she was a steel magnolia.
She thought that was "pretty good"—
        a sweet Southern flower with unshakable will.
Other things they'd called her
      must have appalled her:
          hayseed,
          dabbler,
          unprofessional.
What did she know about matters executive
      or congressional?
But Rosalynn kept on:
      lobbying for a mental health bill,
      against age discrimination;
      hitting the campaign trail.
Believing that she had to try,
      knowing she might fail.
Working nonstop for those in need.
A steel magnolia?
Yes, indeed.

ANNE FRANCES "NANCY" ROBBINS DAVIS REAGAN

(1981–1989)

Her main campaign was Ronnie.
Yes, she took on drug abuse with the phrase
    "Just say no."
She worked hard and traveled far to do her part.
But witness her adoring gaze
    at her presidential beau.
She was his protector,
    his personnel director,
    the shrewd detector
of those who didn't have his best interests at heart.
She'd discreetly persist and get them dismissed.
Some say she was the iron fist
    in the velvet glove.
She made known, like First Ladies before her,
    she did it all for love.

41

BARBARA PIERCE BUSH

(1989–1993)

Was married to a president,
gave birth to another,
said that she resembled
     everyone's grandmother.
Made fun of her weight, her age, her looks.
Strongly believed in the power of books.
Never was a fancy dresser
     like Jacqueline or Betty or her stylish predecessor.
If the press disparaged her, she had a thick skin—
     but a mighty sharp tongue if they criticized her kin.

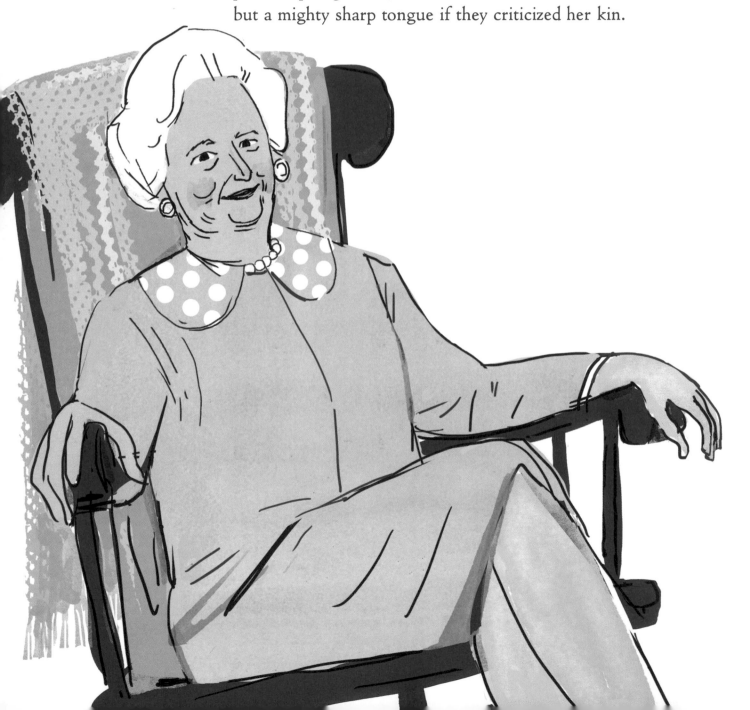

HILLARY DIANE RODHAM CLINTON

(1993–2001)

Firsts for a First Lady:

First to go to Yale, get her degree in law.
First female partner of a firm down in Arkansas.
First with her own office in the coveted West Wing.
First to win a Grammy for her book (she didn't sing).
First to be elected to the U.S. Senate.
With empowerment of women as a major tenet,
      she directed the country's Department of State.
First to be her party's presidential candidate.

And though she lost the race, history will note:
First woman to win the popular vote.

LAURA LANE WELCH BUSH

(2001–2009)

Perhaps what got her through all the elections,
the waiting to see if he'd succeed,
was a love of libraries and their collections,
a chance to take out books and read.

Family literacy was her great cause,
the issue that she chose to push,
a passion that equaled her mother-in-law's
(as well as supporting those two men named Bush).

MICHELLE LaVAUGHN ROBINSON OBAMA

(2009–2017)

None could have imagined when our nation began
    that she would go to Harvard, embody "Yes, we can."
Would criss-cross the country to inspire
    young people to move, to take charge, to Reach Higher?
None would have imagined this descendant of slaves
    would become the First Lady of this multicolored land
and symbolize a history both terrible and grand.

MELANIA [KNAVS] KNAUSS TRUMP

(2017–)

They say, looking out her window at the smokestacks
in that small factory town—
she dreamed of a different fate—
to forge a different life,
to emigrate.
Through modeling she fashioned a dreamer's entrée
to more sophisticated cities,
to the USA.
She learned languages, changed her name,
married into fortune, embraced new fame.
Until many years later, in her inauguration gown,
she was clearly far away from that small factory town.

BEING THE FIRST LADY

"The First Lady is, and always has been, an unpaid public servant elected by one person—her husband."   —Lady Bird Johnson

The U.S. Constitution defines the role of the president, but it says nothing about the role of the First Lady. She is most often the president's spouse, but, in cases where he is a widower or a bachelor, she may be a relative or even the wife of a cabinet member (whom the president has asked to fill the role). For example, Dolley Madison, who was married to then Secretary of State James Madison, served in this position for widower Thomas Jefferson. The First Lady does not draw a salary, but, in 1978, a law officially granted her a budget and a paid staff.

During the early presidencies, people weren't sure what to call the First Lady. The title only came into consistent use during Lucy Hayes's tenure. It became widespread thanks to a popular 1911 play by Charles Nirdlinger entitled *The First in the Land*. Traditionally, the First Lady acts as the White House hostess, seeing to social events, managing domestic affairs, decorating and renovating the executive mansion, and being the model of style and poise. But over the years, our First Ladies have viewed other aspects of the role differently, according to their own interests, personalities, and certain expectations from the public, from their families, from political parties, and from the press. Some have seen it primarily as caring for their husband and children. Others have served as unofficial political advisors to the president. Some have been more openly political themselves.

In the 20th century, First Ladies began to campaign more actively for their spouses. They also took on projects—from disease prevention to women's, children's, and civil rights, from labor relations to environmental concerns, to literacy, and many other issues. And they have been both praised and criticized for their efforts. They may be more or less popular than their husbands, but they were—and still are—both international celebrities and fascinating private individuals.

Having inherited a great amount of land and many slaves from her first husband, MARTHA DANDRIDGE CUSTIS WASHINGTON was a wealthy Southern widow with two children when she married George Washington. The family moved to Washington's home, Mount Vernon, where Martha was known as an excellent hostess and manager. During the long Revolutionary War, she spent every winter with General Washington and his troops at their encampments. Her most famous trip was to Valley Forge, where she helped provide food, clothing, and nursing for the suffering soldiers. One of her most important precedents as First Lady was establishing a weekly reception for anyone who wanted to attend. Guests often referred to her as "Lady Washington" or "Lady Presidentess."

"I have also learned from experience that the greater part of our happiness or misery depends upon our dispositions, and not upon our circumstances." —MW

ABIGAIL SMITH ADAMS kept more than a thousand of the eloquent letters she exchanged with John Adams during their long separations. Published by her grandson, they tell the story of a strong-willed patriot who struggled with running their farm and raising four children, and who urged that the new government give women equal rights. After the Revolutionary War, she joined John on his diplomatic missions to France and Great Britain. She was the first First Lady to live in the still-unfinished White House, and also the first to be both the wife of one president and the mother of another—John Quincy Adams.

"[R]emember the Ladies, and be more generous and favorable to them than your ancestors. Do not put such unlimited power into the hands of the husbands. Remember, all men would be tyrants if they could." —AA

Thomas Jefferson's beloved wife, MARTHA WAYLES SKELTON JEFFERSON, was never actually First Lady—she died nineteen years before he became president. During her lifetime, she managed their plantation, Monticello, and was said to be not only a lively hostess but a fine musician. After giving birth to seven children in fourteen years—only two of whom lived to adulthood—her health deteriorated rapidly. She asked Jefferson never to remarry after her death, and he never did. During his two presidential terms, their daughters occasionally served as hostesses. Eventually, Jefferson asked if his secretary of state's wife would take on the task. She was Dolley Madison—and she was more than happy to accept the job.

"In every scheme of happiness she is placed in the foreground of the picture as the principal figure. Take that away, and there is no picture for me." —TJ on MJ

Serving as Thomas Jefferson's hostess prepared DOLLEY PAYNE TODD MADISON well for the role of First Lady. At her celebrated gatherings, which sometimes featured the ice cream she is said to have popularized, she brought people together, forging social networks and collecting political information to pass along to her husband, James Madison. Dolley became a legend during the War of 1812 by rescuing Gilbert Stuart's famous portrait of George Washington as well as several important government documents. When her husband's presidency ended, the pair retired to his plantation, Montpelier. But upon James's death, Dolley found herself in debt and had to sell Montpelier. Congress gave her an honorary seat and helped her financially by buying Madison's papers. She was also given money by her former household slave, Paul Jennings. Till the end of her life, Dolley was still frequently called upon for advice by incoming First Ladies and was the exemplar by which these women were judged.

"I would rather fight with my hands than my tongue." —DM

In 1794, during the French Revolution, James Monroe was appointed Minister to France. His young wife, ELIZABETH KORTRIGHT MONROE, accompanied him and became so popular there that she was called "la belle Americaine"—the beautiful American. She used her position to visit Madame Lafayette, wife of the Marquis de Lafayette, a French aristocrat and officer who fought against the British during the American Revolution. Madame Lafayette was going to be executed, but because of Elizabeth's interest, she was spared. As First Lady, Elizabeth brought European formality to the White House, which did not endear her to Americans.

Louisa Catherine Adams, wife of John Quincy Adams, in a letter to John Adams: "She was dressed . . . in the highest style of fashion and moved not like a Queen (for that is an unpardonable word in this country) but like a goddess."

Born in England and educated in France, LOUISA CATHERINE JOHNSON ADAMS was the first of two First Ladies not originally from the U.S. Intelligent and sophisticated, she accompanied her husband, John Quincy Adams, on his diplomatic posts, which sometimes led to dangerous journeys. The most perilous was a forty-day carriage ride that she and their young son, Charles, took during the winter from Russia across war-torn Europe to join Adams in France. During his run for president, Louisa acted as her husband's manager, using her social power to advance his campaign. But once he was elected, he rarely sought her advice. She penned an unpublished autobiography entitled *Adventures of a Nobody*. After John Quincy's presidency ended, the couple grew closer. He became an esteemed U.S. representative and collaborated with Louisa to speak out against slavery. When she died four years after him, Congress, in a show of great respect, adjourned so that members could attend her funeral.

"I have nothing to do with the disposal of affairs and have never but once been consulted." —LA

RACHEL DONELSON ROBARDS JACKSON had an unhappy first marriage. She thought that she was legally divorced when she married Andrew Jackson. It turned out that her first husband, Lewis Robards, had never signed the papers. Eventually, Robards did divorce her, but Jackson's opponents used the scandal against him in the election campaign of 1824 (which he lost) and of 1828 (which he won). Rachel died before her husband's inauguration and was buried in the gown she intended to wear. Jackson was devastated. After a long period of mourning, he asked her favorite niece, and later on his daughter-in-law, to serve as hostess at the White House.

"I would rather be a doorkeeper in the house of God than live in that palace at Washington." —RJ

Not much is known about Martin Van Buren's wife, HANNAH HOES VAN BUREN. Quiet and religious, she spoke Dutch and was his childhood sweetheart. They were married for twelve years, during which time she gave birth to six children, four of whom survived. She died while her children were still young, eighteen years before Van Buren became president. He did not mention her at all in his autobiography nor apparently did he discuss her with their children, possibly because it would have been considered impolite and also perhaps because of his great grief. He never remarried nor did he have a daughter, so his eldest son Abraham's wife, Angelica Van Buren, served as hostess during part of his term. She tried to make the office of First Lady more royal by greeting guests on a throne-like platform. It did not go over well, and the platform was soon removed.

The Albany Argus (newspaper) on Hannah Hoes Van Buren: "An ornament of the Christian faith."

ANNA TUTHILL SYMMES HARRISON's father did not want her to wed Lt. William Henry Harrison and endure the life of a military wife, so the pair married in secret. In 1811, while he was governor of the Indiana territory, Harrison clashed with Indian forces at the Battle of Tippecanoe. To keep her family out of danger, Anna moved with her children to her parents' home in Ohio, where she remained during Harrison's terms as congressman, senator, and foreign minister to Colombia. William retired from politics in 1829. Seven years later, he was pressed to run for president. When he won, Anna was too ill to go to his inauguration. One month later, as she was packing to join him, he died in office. Anna became the first presidential widow to receive a pension. She outlived all but one of her ten children and helped raise her grandson, Benjamin Harrison, who would also become president.

"I wish that my husband's friends had left him where he is, happy and contented in retirement." —AH

During her marriage to John Tyler, LETITIA CHRISTIAN TYLER had managed a plantation and given birth to seven surviving children. But she had been in poor health for several years when, following the death of William Henry Harrison, her husband unexpectedly became president. Letitia directed the White House's domestic affairs mainly from her bedroom and took part in few social events. She was the first First Lady to die in the White House.

Daughter-in-law Priscilla Cooper Tyler on Letitia Tyler: "The most entirely unselfish person you can imagine."

A wealthy Northerner whose family had once owned slaves and to this day still owns Gardiners Island in New York, JULIA GARDINER TYLER sympathized with the South. At a White House event, Julia caught John Tyler's eye and he courted her. During the shipboard explosion in which her father was killed, Julia fainted into Tyler's arms and shortly thereafter they were wed. Julia adored being First Lady. She threw lavish parties, lobbied officials on behalf of friends and relatives, and actively promoted Tyler's proposal to annex Texas. Thirty years younger than her husband, Julia gave birth to seven children. Two of her grandchildren survived into the 21st century. After the Civil War, she was left impoverished by the defeat of the Confederacy and fought to get a pension from Congress. She provided her own biography to Laura Holloway, who compiled the first comprehensive book on First Ladies. To the end of her days, she called herself "Mrs. Ex-President Tyler."

"I have commenced my auspicious reign and am in quiet possession of the Presidential Mansion. . . . [T]his winter I intend to do something in the way of entertaining that shall be the admiration and talk of all Washington world." —JGT

Well educated and childless, SARAH WHITSETT CHILDRESS POLK had the brains and the time to serve James K. Polk as his assistant, helping with his speeches and correspondence, giving him advice on political issues, and keeping callers out of his way. She agreed with James that the country had the right to expand, even if it meant taking land from Native Americans—a policy called "Manifest Destiny." Although she believed that women should have higher learning and not be limited to housekeeping, she did not support the women's rights activists who gathered at the Seneca Falls Convention in 1848. A devout Presbyterian, she would not dance, drink, attend horse races, or go to the theater. Despite her strict moral code, she believed that the South would collapse without slavery and she owned several slaves herself. James died three months after leaving the White House, and Sarah remained a widow, uninvolved in politics, for the next forty-two years.

"If I should be so fortunate as to reach the White House, I expect to live on twenty-five thousand dollars a year, and I will neither keep house nor make butter." —SP

For nearly forty years, MARGARET "PEGGY" MACKALL SMITH TAYLOR, the daughter of a wealthy plantation-owning family, followed her husband, Zachary Taylor, from one frontier garrison to another. Zachary had no background in politics, but he was a hero of the Mexican War and his party nominated him for the presidency. Peggy did not want him to run, nor did she want to be First Lady. She refused to take part in any of the social functions at the White House, giving the role of hostess to her daughter, Betty Bliss. Rumors circulated that Peggy was a crude, pipe-smoking recluse—all of which was untrue. Less than two years into his term, Zachary died suddenly. Peggy died two years later.

Zachary Taylor on Margaret Taylor: "You know, my wife was as much of a soldier as I was."

Millard Fillmore, aged nineteen, fell in love with his twenty-one-year-old teacher, who would later become his wife—ABIGAIL POWERS FILLMORE. When he set up law practice in Buffalo, New York, the pair established a college and a lending library there. As First Lady, Abigail started another library—in the Yellow Oval Room of the White House. She used the room as a salon where she entertained musicians, statesmen, writers, and other luminaries of the day. After serving one term, Fillmore was succeeded by Franklin Pierce. Suffering from chronically poor health, Abigail accompanied her husband on a raw day to Pierce's inauguration. She caught pneumonia and died a few weeks later.

Abigail Fillmore, after a discussion with a theologian: "I do not recollect when I had such a mental treat."

JANE MEANS APPLETON PIERCE loved her husband and hated his political ambitions. While Franklin Pierce was in Congress, she returned to their home state of New Hampshire. She suffered emotionally from their separation and from the deaths of their first two sons. In the early 1840s, she was relieved when they had a third son, Benny, and Franklin agreed to retire from politics. But in 1852, Franklin was nominated for the presidency. Then, two months before Pierce's inauguration, during a railroad accident, Benny was killed right before his parents' eyes. For her first two years in the White House, Jane did not attend any social events. She felt that God was punishing her and she spent much time praying and writing letters to her dead son, asking for his forgiveness. Though both Jane and Franklin were anti-slavery, he was in favor of preserving the Union, even if it meant allowing slavery in the South, while she was for ending slavery once and for all. She lived to see the Civil War begin—but not to see it end.

"My mind is sometimes, yes much of the time in a perfect chaos, and I hardly know what I think or feel, or whether I feel at all." —JP

Orphaned at a young age, HARRIET "HAL" REBECCA LANE (JOHNSTON) became the ward of her uncle, James Buchanan, whom she affectionately called "Nunc." Buchanan was our only bachelor president, and he made poised and vivacious Harriet his hostess. During his presidency, tensions were increasing between the North and the South. Harriet, nicknamed "Hal," was talented at complex seating arrangements and keeping the peace between factions at White House social events. An avid art collector, Hal willed her collection to the government and is credited with being a founder of the Smithsonian Institution's National Gallery of Art. She also endowed a home for invalid children, which today is known as the Harriet Lane Clinic at Johns Hopkins Hospital.

"Uncle places so much confidence in me that he gives himself no uneasiness." —HL

Shrewish, gracious, spiteful, caring, self-centered, supportive—all of these words and more have been applied to MARY ANNE TODD LINCOLN. She and Abraham Lincoln had a stormy courtship and even broke off their engagement before they eventually married. He respected her advice, but was angered by her spending sprees, which left them in debt—her purchases of "flub-dubs" to redecorate the White House while soldiers were in need of blankets and food. She also bought many dresses made by Elizabeth Keckley, a former slave, who wrote a memoir about the First Lady. Because her Kentuckian family owned slaves, Mary was accused of being both a Southern spy and a traitor to the Southern cause during the Civil War. But she was also seen as an angel of mercy by the soldiers she nursed. Mary was devastated by her son Willie's death and her husband's assassination. When a second son, Tad, died in 1871, Mary had a breakdown. Her eldest son, Robert, had her committed to an insane asylum. With the help of one of the nation's first female lawyers, she won her release. She spent the last years of her life in her sister's home in Springfield, Illinois, where she'd married Abraham Lincoln forty years before.

"To keep up appearances, I must have money—more than Mr. Lincoln can spare for me. He is too honest to make a penny outside of his salary; consequently I had, and still have, no alternative but to run in debt." —ML

To supplement her shoemaker father's meager income, ELIZA MCCARDLE JOHNSON, with her mother, made sandals and quilts to sell. Andrew Johnson was a tailor when they met. Better educated than he, Eliza taught him writing and arithmetic and also helped him become a good public speaker. He rose quickly in politics and was elected a U.S. senator from their native Tennessee, and later on, vice president. When Tennessee joined the Confederacy, Eliza helped smuggle food to Union soldiers hiding in the mountains and became a refugee, seeking shelter from strangers until she and their family were finally able to join Andrew in Nashville. Following Lincoln's assassination, Johnson became president, but Eliza was too ill with tuberculosis to preside over social events. Her daughter, Martha Patterson, took on the role of official hostess. When Johnson was impeached in 1868, Eliza never ceased to believe that he would be acquitted. She was right: by a single vote, he was able to remain in office.

"It's all very well for those who like it, but I do not like this public life at all." —EJ

JULIA BOGGS DENT GRANT's father did not want her to marry her brother's West Point roommate, Ulysses S. Grant, but he eventually gave his consent. Before the Civil War, Julia enjoyed the social whirl of army life. After the war, she relished being married to a victorious hero. She was even more delighted to become First Lady. She brought elegance and luxury to the White House, restoring social life to Washington. She was upset when "Ulys," as she called him, refused to run for a third term, and wanted to stay on in the executive mansion until the contested election between Rutherford B. Hayes and Samuel Tilden was settled. The story goes that she wept upon leaving the White House for the final time.

"My life in the White House was like a bright and beautiful dream." —JG

LUCY WARE WEBB HAYES was the first First Lady to have a college degree. Her husband, Rutherford B. Hayes, had been a popular three-term governor of Ohio, and Lucy was experienced at being a politician's spouse. A staunch abolitionist and supporter of higher education for women (but not their right to vote), Lucy, as First Lady, was publicly silent about her beliefs for fear of harming her husband's career. She chose instead to focus on him, their children, and their menagerie of pets. Although she wanted to set a moral example for the nation, she refused to become the public advocate of the Woman's Christian Temperance Union (WCTU). Later generations would mockingly refer to her as "Lemonade Lucy," but it was actually Rutherford who forbade hard liquor in the White House. Lucy was in fact against prohibition.

"A woman's mind is as strong as a man's. . . . [S]he is considered his equal in all things and his superior in some." —LH

LUCRETIA "CRETE" RUDOLPH GARFIELD spoke four languages and taught French, Latin, and algebra. Concerned about compromising her privacy, she warily gave her approval when James Garfield said he would not run for president without it. She helped him conduct the nation's first "front porch" campaigns during which the candidate literally spoke from his porch to large groups of voters. She lobbied Congress for funds to renovate the White House, which was in a state of disrepair, and gave interviews to the press, making her political positions known. When James Garfield was shot by Charles Guiteau, a deranged supporter of a faction that supported civil service reform, Crete nursed him for more than two months until he died. The press hailed her as a role model for her strength and optimism. Crete spent the rest of her thirty-six years quietly, preserving her husband's name and career, learning about engineering and architecture, and helping to design her home in Pasadena, California.

A newspaper journalist on Lucretia Garfield: "The wife of the President is the bravest woman in the universe."

ELLEN "NELL" LEWIS HERNDON ARTHUR sang in the choir at St. John's Episcopal Church in Washington, D.C., and was known for her beautiful voice. In 1857, she became engaged to Chester ("Chet") A. Arthur, who was establishing a law practice in New York. He sent her a letter describing "the soft, moonlight nights of June . . . the golden, fleeting hours at Lake George" that they had spent together. In January 1880, Nell developed pneumonia and died. Arthur was still mourning her death when he became vice president—and then president, following James Garfield's assassination in 1881. He had a stained glass window made in her memory and set in St. John's Episcopal Church so that he could view it from the White House every night.

Chester A. Arthur, upon accepting the nomination for vice president shortly after his wife's death:
"Honors to me now are not what they once were."

Grover Cleveland entered the White House as a bachelor. He appeared to be courting his law partner's widow. Instead, at the age of forty-eight, he married her twenty-one-year-old daughter for whom he'd once bought a baby carriage. The beautiful and intelligent FRANCES CLARA FOLSOM CLEVELAND (PRESTON) became so popular and received so many fan letters that she had to hire a social secretary to answer them. She lent her support to several charitable institutions to help African American women and children and invited working women to the White House. Businesses used her image to sell many products, often without her permission. Cleveland served one term, then lost the next election, but Frances was convinced that they'd be back in the White House four years later, and they were. By then, the couple had a child—Baby Ruth, for whom some claim the candy bar was named. During Cleveland's second term, Frances gave birth to two more daughters, one of whom was actually born in the White House. In 1913, five years after Grover's death, Frances married Thomas J. Preston, Jr., a professor of archaeology at Wells College, her alma mater, where she was a trustee.

"These people sent me a box with their perfumes, for which I thanked them,
and now they're advertising their face powder as being used by me, also. Can you have it taken out?" —FC

For CAROLINE LAVINIA SCOTT HARRISON, Frances Cleveland was a hard act to follow. The press portrayed Caroline as old-fashioned, but in fact she was more progressive in terms of women's rights than her predecessor. She agreed to raise funds for the Johns Hopkins School of Medicine on the condition that women be admitted. She became the first president general of the Daughters of the American Revolution (DAR), which she felt could become a political force for women. Caroline also came up with a plan to renovate the White House by creating two wings—an East Wing for the living quarters and a West Wing for the office—but Congress would not authorize the expense. In 1892, she died in the White House before Harrison lost his bid for re-election. Years later, under Theodore Roosevelt's administration, her plans for the White House renovation finally came to pass, although a bit more modestly.

"I am disgusted with newspapers and reporters. Truth is a characteristic entirely unknown to them." —CH

A bank manager and a world traveler, she'd been a lively young woman when William McKinley married her. But by the time she became First Lady, IDA SAXTON MCKINLEY was disabled, prone to seizures and other ailments. Doctors gave her medications, which made her listless and moody. In addition, she suffered depression from the loss of her grandparents, mother, and two children. Sometimes, if she had a seizure at dinner, William would place a napkin over her face until she recovered. She was able to greet some visitors at public receptions, but entertained others, including Susan B. Anthony and fellow suffragists whom Ida supported, in her private suite. Though she spent much of her time indoors, she was able to take several tours with her husband. She was in Buffalo, but not present at the Pan-American Exposition there, when he was shot by anarchist Leon Czolgosz on September 9, 1901. Showing great physical and emotional strength, she cared for her husband during the last days of his life and attended his funeral—without the aid of any medication.

Ida McKinley, on having to share her husband's open coffin with the public in the Canton, Ohio, City Hall:
"I want him one last night in this house alone with me, so I could look at him one more time."

EDITH KERMIT CAROW ROOSEVELT and Theodore "T. R." Roosevelt (called "Teddy" by the press and general public) were childhood friends. After his first wife, Alice Lee, died, leaving him with an infant also named Alice, T. R. and Edith married. Edith asked to raise Alice, and, over the next ten years, had five children of her own. Throughout his career, T. R. held many offices, and Edith displayed great aptitude as the wife of a public official. She was adept at packing up the children and moving to their many different lodgings—one of which turned out to be the White House. When William McKinley was killed and Roosevelt became president, Edith was suddenly thrust into the role of First Lady. With Caroline Harrison's plans as the basis for renovation, and with Congress now willing to supply the funds, she was able to remodel the executive mansion. Roosevelt had sworn to be a one-term president, but because he disagreed with the policies of his chosen Republican successor, William Howard Taft, he ran against Taft in the 1912 election on the Progressive (Bullmoose) Party ticket. That split the vote, allowing Democrat Woodrow Wilson, whom Edith disliked, to win.

"Nothing would please me more than when I die they put this inscription on my tombstone: 'Everything she did was for the happiness of others.'" —ER

When HELEN "NELLIE" LOUISE HERRON TAFT visited the White House at age sixteen, she decided that she would someday live there—as the president's wife. One year later, she met "Will"—William Howard Taft. She urged him to become governor-general of the Philippines. She also counseled Will to put on hold his greatest ambition to be a Supreme Court justice and instead become the Republican candidate for president. Nellie was the first First Lady to ride beside her husband at his inauguration. Two months later, she had a stroke, but with fierce determination, she rebounded. She was an advocate for women's suffrage and workers' rights. Resolved to beautify Washington, she had cherry trees planted in the city—a lasting legacy. She also started the First Ladies' inaugural gowns collection at the Smithsonian Institution. Nellie had long suspected that Roosevelt might run against her husband. Wilson's win allowed Taft to become chief justice of the Supreme Court.

"I had always had the satisfaction of knowing almost as much as [William Howard Taft] about the politics and intricacies of any situation. I think any woman can discuss with her husband topics of national interest." —NT

Before her marriage to Woodrow Wilson, ELLEN LOUISE AXSON WILSON had studied art and exhibited work in several shows. When Woodrow became president of the United States, Ellen added the now-famous Rose Garden, the setting for many presidential ceremonies, to the White House. A descendant of a slave-holding family, Ellen became interested in social reform—particularly in improving Washington's slums, which were largely inhabited by Black people. Suffering from a kidney ailment, she died in the White House. As a tribute to her, Congress passed the "alley bill" to demolish the slums, but it was not implemented until Eleanor Roosevelt took up the cause many years later.

"Ah! But I am ambitious! And the best of it is that mine is gratified ambition, for I am ambitious for you—and for myself, too." —EW

Widow EDITH BOLLING GALT WILSON met Woodrow Wilson while he was still in mourning for the wife he adored. They were married a year after Ellen Wilson's death. Edith felt that her main role was to advise Woodrow and to keep him healthy during the difficult build-up to World War I. She supported the war effort in many ways: she decoded messages and set an example for economizing, even bringing sheep to the White House lawn to graze and then selling the wool to raise funds. She was the first sitting First Lady to join her husband in Europe to meet the troops. After the war, the president suffered a stroke. Edith disguised Woodrow's disability from his cabinet and the press. She decided who could visit him and which issues should be brought to his attention. When visitors were allowed to call on him, Edith and his doctor positioned Wilson so that people could not see his paralyzed side. After his death in 1924, she spent the rest of her life managing and promoting her husband's legacy.

"I am not thinking of the country now, I am thinking of my husband." —EW

Abandoned by her first husband, FLORENCE MABEL KLING HARDING supported herself and her young son by teaching piano. She met Warren G. Harding when he was the editor of the *Marion Daily Star*. After they married, she took over the newspaper's accounts and showed a great gift for business. Warren was a good speaker and Florence urged him to go into politics. Women finally had the right to vote, and Florence worked to get them to vote for Warren for president. After his election, Florence advised him on speeches and cabinet appointments, often sitting in on cabinet meetings herself.

She created "photo ops," brought jazz and movies to the White House, and was the first First Lady to fly in a plane. When political scandals began to surface, she joined Harding on his cross-country "Voyage of Understanding" to meet and speak with citizens. She was with him when he died suddenly in San Francisco. To protect his image, she burned many documents and letters. She also refused to allow an autopsy, leading to accusations that she'd poisoned him—charges that have been discredited.

"I know what's best for the President. I put him in the White House. He does well when he listens to me and poorly when he does not." —FH

Calvin Coolidge did not want his wife to wear trousers, bob her hair, fly in a plane, drive a car, or speak to the press. He believed in being frugal—except when it came to his wife's clothes. As a result, gracious and outgoing GRACE ANNA GOODHUE COOLIDGE became so fashionable that she received an award for style from the French garment industry. Before becoming a First Lady, Grace taught lip-reading to the deaf and was an ardent athlete. As First Lady, she hosted receptions and other events, and was largely removed from politics. A rabid baseball fan, she listened to games on the radio and frequently attended them, giving her the nickname "First Lady of Baseball." When her son died of blood poisoning at the age of sixteen, she carried on her duties with dignity. After Calvin's death, Grace became a trustee of the Clarke School for the Deaf. She took her first plane ride and her first trip to Europe. She also cut her hair, learned to drive, and wore her first pair of pants.

"This was I and yet, not I. This was the wife of the President of the United States and she took precedence over me." —GC

Adventurous, athletic, and able to speak five languages, LOU HENRY HOOVER met Herbert "Bert" Hoover at Stanford University, where they were both studying geology. Because she was a woman, Lou could not get a job in the field. But Bert became a mining engineer, which made him wealthy. During World War I, Lou was strongly involved in relief efforts, and for most of her life, she worked with the Girl Scouts and other groups encouraging young women to pursue outdoor activities. As First Lady, she gave lavish parties, which she and Bert paid for. To a public struggling to survive during the Depression, the Hoovers' behavior appeared unseemly. Lou, like her husband, advocated "volunteerism"—individuals and businesses donating money and time to others—rather than large-scale government intervention. She did, in fact, contribute huge amounts to charities, pay her secretaries' salaries, and host relief efforts, without advertising her role to the press. After her death, Herbert discovered thousands of checks from people repaying the loans Lou had given them during the Depression. She'd never cashed them.

"Every young girl should have the opportunity of learning out-of-doors by first-hand observation." —LH

The niece of President Theodore Roosevelt, ANNA ELEANOR ROOSEVELT was influenced at a young age by her uncle's involvement in social reform. She married her distant cousin, Franklin Delano Roosevelt, at the age of twenty, gave birth to five surviving children, developed an interest in politics, and began her career in radio broadcasting. When Japan bombed Pearl Harbor, leading to America's entry into World War II, it was Eleanor who addressed the nation first. She was not eager to become First Lady, but she soon transformed the role. She held press conferences at which only female reporters were allowed, and wrote books, articles, and a daily newspaper column called "My Day." Traveling the nation, she inspected the New Deal projects her husband had initiated to help get the country out of the Depression, and she worked to achieve civil rights for women and for Black people, becoming the first white person in Washington, D.C., to join both the National Association for the Advancement of Colored People (NAACP) and the National Urban League. After FDR died during his fourth term, Eleanor, who'd served longer than any other First Lady, became a delegate to the newly formed United Nations, where she drafted the Universal Declaration of Human Rights. She continued working for human rights until her death in 1962.

"If you are interested, you never have to look for new interests. They come to you." —ER

ELIZABETH "BESS" VIRGINIA WALLACE TRUMAN preferred life in her hometown of Independence, Missouri, to the Washington, D.C., spotlight, but she campaigned for her husband across the country when he was running for vice president. At every stop, he referred to her as the "Boss" (and to their daughter, Margaret, as the "Boss's Boss"). When FDR died in office and Truman became president, Bess chose to keep a low profile as First Lady. However, in private, she served as Harry's confidante and advisor, reading the *Congressional Record* and editing his speeches. When many politicians, reporters, and citizens said that the deteriorating White House should be torn down and replaced, she lobbied Congress to preserve and renovate the original structure—a process that was more expensive—and she won. After Truman's term ended, she was glad to return permanently to Missouri. She died there ten years after Harry at the age of ninety-seven—the longest-lived of all our First Ladies.

"A woman's place in public is to sit beside her husband, be silent, and be sure her hat is on straight." —BT

MAMIE GENEVA DOUD EISENHOWER went from a comfortable debutante's life to that of a military wife. She once estimated that, in thirty-seven years, she'd changed households at least twenty-seven times. A war hero, Dwight David "Ike" Eisenhower was a popular candidate for president—and Mamie was a popular candidate's spouse. She felt that women should not pursue careers outside of marriage and saw the role of First Lady as being a wife and a hostess. However, she also believed that that role entitled her to invite whomever she wanted to the White House. The 4-H Club Camp for Negro Boys and Girls was welcome. Senator Joseph McCarthy, infamous for his anti-communist crusade, was not. After Ike suffered a heart attack, Mamie became the national chairperson for the American Heart Association, raising money and encouraging volunteers. When he died in 1969, Mamie spent her remaining years at their farm in Gettysburg, Pennsylvania—the first and only permanent home the Eisenhowers ever owned.

"Ike runs the country, and I turn the pork chops." —ME

Educated in private schools and at the Sorbonne University in Paris, JACQUELINE LEE BOUVIER KENNEDY (ONASSIS) won awards for her writing, and after graduation she became the *Washington Times-Herald*'s "inquiring photographer." Among her interviewees was Senator John F. Kennedy. The pair married in 1953 and had two surviving children, John Jr. and Caroline. As First Lady, Jacqueline was the epitome of glamour and sophistication, whose hairstyle and clothes were copied by many. One of her priorities was restoring the White House, turning it into a museum of American history and decorative arts open to the public. Her televised tour of the refurbished mansion was watched by over fifty million viewers. She pushed for the establishment of the National Cultural Center, now known as the Kennedy Center, in Washington, D.C. On November 22, 1963, she was riding next to her husband in an open car in Dallas, Texas, when he was assassinated. People around the world admired her dignity during his funeral. Five years later, she married shipping magnate Aristotle Onassis and became an editor for the publishing company Viking Press, then for Doubleday. When she died in 1994, her son, John Jr., described her three most important traits: "her love of words, the bonds of home and family, and her spirit of adventure."

"What is sad for women of my generation is that they weren't supposed to work if they had families.
What were they going to do when the children are grown—watch the raindrops coming down the window pane?" —JK

When Lyndon Johnson was thrust into the role of president, CLAUDIA ALTA "LADY BIRD" TAYLOR JOHNSON said that she felt she was onstage for a part she hadn't rehearsed. In fact, she was well prepared indeed. She'd run her husband's congressional office during World War II, and she'd also managed her own radio station. When Johnson, then Senate majority leader, had a heart attack, Lady Bird acted as his gatekeeper, reviewing with his staff the concerns he needed to address. During Lyndon's 1964 campaign for the presidency, she championed his projects—particularly the Civil Rights Act—touring the South by a train called the "Lady Bird Special" to garner support. Making environmentalism her own initiative, she pushed for planting flowers and creating parks in Washington, D.C., lobbied for the Highway Beautification Act to remove unsightly billboards around the country, and advocated for protection of wilderness preserves and for anti-pollution legislation. After Johnson left office, Lady Bird created the National Wildflower Research Center, renamed the Lady Bird Johnson Wildflower Center, in Austin, Texas. She was given the Medal of Freedom and the Congressional Gold Medal by Presidents Gerald Ford and Ronald Reagan.

"The environment is where we all meet; where all have a mutual interest; it is the one thing all of us share.
It is not only a mirror of ourselves, but a focusing lens on what we can become." —LBJ

THELMA CATHERINE "PAT" RYAN NIXON's family owned a truck farm, and as a child, she helped with planting and harvesting vegetables. After losing both parents, she continued to hold many jobs to support herself. She met Richard "Dick" Nixon when they were performing at a community theater. President Eisenhower considered her an excellent goodwill ambassador and sent her with Vice President Nixon to over fifty countries. As First Lady, she accompanied Nixon on his historic visit to China. In her honor, the Chinese government sent two pandas to the National Zoo. Though she had strong views, which included supporting the Equal Rights Amendment (ERA) and the inclusion of women on the Supreme Court, Pat was not consulted by Dick in his policy decisions. Refusing to believe he had anything to do with the break-in at the Democratic National Committee headquarters, she remained loyal to her husband during the Watergate scandal. After his resignation from office, which she'd advised against, she made few public appearances, nursed Nixon through his illnesses and depression, and never joined him on any of his four visits to the White House.

"I have sacrificed everything in my life that I consider precious in order to advance the political career of my husband." —PN

ELIZABETH "BETTY" ANN BLOOMER WARREN FORD was surprised when her husband, Congressman Gerald "Jerry" Ford, was appointed vice president after Spiro Agnew, President Nixon's vice president, resigned—and even more so when Nixon also resigned and Jerry became chief executive. A former model, a dancer who'd performed with the famous Martha Graham Dance Company, and the mother of four children, Betty became an outspoken First Lady during her husband's time in office. She came out in favor of controversial women's issues, including the ERA and the *Roe v. Wade* decision, which legalized abortion. In 1974, she broke the news about her breast cancer—a condition that was not openly discussed at the time. As a result, many women chose to have themselves screened for the disease. Betty was equally frank about her struggles with alcoholism and addiction to painkillers. She co-founded what is now the Betty Ford Center for rehabilitation. Presidential historian Richard Norton Smith said, "In the end, simply by being herself, she made it easier for millions of American women to be themselves."

About becoming First Lady at Nixon's resignation: "I figured, okay, I'll move to the White House,
do the best I can, and if they don't like it, they can kick me out. But they can't make me be somebody I'm not." —BF

For her gracious Southern manner and her strong will, ELEANOR ROSALYNN SMITH CARTER was labeled a "steel magnolia." When Jimmy Carter won the presidential election, Rosalynn reorganized the Office of the First Lady into four departments and hired more staff. Calling her his "secret weapon," Carter asked her to sit in on cabinet meetings and some national security briefings, and he sent her as his envoy to Latin America to discuss his issues directly with leaders there. She became honorary chair of the President's Commission on Mental Health, supported the ERA (which did not pass), and lobbied on behalf of senior citizens to abolish age discrimination in the workplace. Today, she chairs the Carter Center's Mental Health Task Force and is involved with Habitat for Humanity, an organization that builds homes for the needy.

"I don't think that any man who would be President of the United States would have a wife with no ambition, who'd just sit and do nothing." —RC

ANNE FRANCES "NANCY" ROBBINS DAVIS REAGAN was an actor. She met Ronald Reagan when he was president of the Screen Actors Guild. In 1956, they appeared in one movie together—*Hellcats of the Navy*. It was her last film. During Reagan's term as governor of California, she lobbied against teen drug abuse. When Ronnie, as she called him, won the presidential election against Jimmy Carter, she expanded her efforts against drug abuse into her "Just Say No" campaign. Criticized for undertaking an expensive renovation of the White House and for wearing designer clothes during a recession, she worked to repair her image by poking fun at herself. After an attempt on Reagan's life in 1981, Nancy became his greatest champion and protector. She pushed to replace members of his staff whom she felt did not have his best interests at heart. When he was stricken with Alzheimer's disease, Nancy became his caretaker until his death in 2004. She became a strong supporter of embryonic stem cell research in hope that it might lead to a cure for this disease.

"However the first lady fits in, she has a unique and important role to play in looking after her husband. And it's only natural that she'll let him know what she thinks. I always did that for Ronnie, and I always will." —NR

A native New Yorker, BARBARA PIERCE BUSH was just sixteen when she met George Herbert Walker Bush. They had six children, one of whom, Robin, died of leukemia. Barbara has said that Robin's death caused her hair to turn white. When Bush became vice president, Barbara chose to promote literacy. As First Lady, she continued to make that a major cause. Although she did not involve herself publicly in her husband's political issues, she spoke out against bigotry in an interview with *Ebony* magazine and made the news when, attempting to dispel fears about the disease, she held a baby infected with AIDS. She was able to make jokes at her own expense about her style, her weight, and her hair, but if anyone attacked her husband, her son, President George W. Bush, or her other children, she'd rise to their defense. At Wellesley College, students protested her appearance as the commencement speaker because they felt that she defined herself through her husband's achievements. She chose to speak anyway, ending her talk with "Who knows? Somewhere out in this audience may even be someone who will one day follow in my footsteps and preside over the White House as the president's spouse. And I wish *him* well."

"I know truthfully that every single problem in America would be better if more people could read, write and comprehend." —BB

Interested in politics and in social reform at an early age, HILLARY DIANE RODHAM CLINTON graduated from Yale Law School—where she met Bill Clinton—and became a staff attorney for the Children's Defense Fund, which works to improve policies and programs for the nation's children. The Clintons were faculty members at the University of Arkansas law school. They married in 1975 and had a daughter, Chelsea, five years later. Hillary joined the prestigious Rose Law Firm, where she eventually became a full partner. When Bill was elected president, he told the public they'd be getting "two for the price of one." Hillary set up an office in the White House's West Wing—the only First Lady to do so—and Bill appointed her to head a task force on health care reform, an effort that failed. She continued to support children's and women's issues both at home and abroad, and she helped create the Department of Justice's Violence Against Women office. She wrote several books, one of which, *It Takes a Village*, won a Spoken Word Grammy Award. After Clinton left office, Hillary became a U.S. Senator from New York, ran a vigorous campaign for presidential candidate, and then served as President Obama's secretary of state. In 2016, she was the Democratic nominee for president. She lost the election, though she won the popular vote.

"It is past time for women to take their rightful place, side by side with men, in the rooms where the fates of peoples, where their children's and grandchildren's fates, are decided." —HC

LAURA LANE WELCH BUSH's love of reading led to her becoming an elementary school teacher and then a librarian. When she married George W. Bush in 1977, she left her job and worked on his unsuccessful congressional campaign. When George became governor of Texas, she promoted literacy programs and started the Texas Book Festival, which raises money to purchase books for the state library system. When George ran for president, Laura did not want to give speeches—but she ultimately made hundreds of them. Two months after the terrorist attacks on September 11, 2001, she became the first First Lady to deliver the president's weekly radio address, speaking about the treatment of women and children in Afghanistan. Continuing to focus on education and literacy, she established the National Book Festival in Washington, D.C. She also traveled extensively to Africa to raise awareness of AIDS and malaria. Since leaving the White House, she has written several books and continues to promote educational causes, as well as women's health issues.

"The power of a book lies in its power to turn a solitary act into a shared vision. As long as we have books, we are not alone." —LB

MICHELLE LAVAUGHN ROBINSON OBAMA went to the first "magnet" high school for gifted children in Chicago, followed by Princeton University and then Harvard Law School. While working as an associate attorney at the firm of Sidley & Austin in 1989, she was the advisor to a new intern—Barack Obama. They married three years later. She moved from law to public service and was vice president of community relations at the University of Chicago Medical Center when Barack decided to run for president. Although she helped him campaign, Michelle limited her time away so that she could be with their two young daughters, Sasha and Malia. She started a vegetable garden at the White House and chose to endorse issues such as healthier eating and physical fitness. In 2014, she launched Reach Higher to encourage young people to continue their education past high school. Today, she is proof that this country has come a long way from the days when it was illegal for Black people to get an education, let alone become president and First Lady of the United States.

"You may not always have a comfortable life and you will not always be able to solve all of the world's problems at once, but don't ever underestimate the importance you can have, because history has shown us that courage can be contagious and hope can take on a life of its own." —MO

Born in Slovenia and fluent in several languages, MELANIA (KNAVS) KNAUSS TRUMP began a modeling career at the age of sixteen. After modeling for fashion houses in Paris and Milan, she moved to New York City in 1996 to advance her vocation, eventually appearing in magazines such as *Vogue, Vanity Fair,* and *Sports Illustrated.* In 1998, she met her future husband, Donald Trump, at a Fashion Week party. They were married seven years later. The following year, Melania gave birth to their son, Barron, and also became a U.S. citizen. Although she did speak at the Republican National Convention, she did not take an active role in her husband's campaign for president. The second foreign-born woman to become First Lady, she has said that her focus will be to help women and children and to combat cyber-bullying.

"After living and working in Milan and Paris, I arrived in New York City twenty years ago, and I saw both the joys and the hardships of daily life. On July 28, 2006, I was very proud to become a citizen of the United States—the greatest privilege on planet Earth." —MT

SOURCES

BOOKS

Black, Allida. *The First Ladies of the United States Of America.* Washington, D.C.: The White House Historical Association, 2013.

Gould, Lewis, ed. *American First Ladies: Their Lives and Their Legacy.* New York: Routledge Publishing, 2001.

Graddy, Lisa Kathleen, and Amy Pastan. *The Smithsonian First Ladies Collection.* Washington, D.C.: Smithsonian Books, 2014.

O'Brien, Cormac. *Secret Lives of the First Ladies.* Philadelphia, Penn.: Quirk Books, 2009.

Pastan, Amy. *First Ladies.* New York: DK Publishing, 2009.

Schneider, Dorothy, and Carl J. Schneider. *First Ladies: A Biographical Dictionary.* New York: Facts on File, 2010.

WEBSITES

http://www.firstladies.org/biographies/

http://firstladies.c-span.org/

http://www.georgewbushlibrary.smu.edu/The-President-and-Family/Laura-W-Bush/The-First-Lady-and-Her-Role.aspx

http://www.history.com/topics/first-ladies

http://history.howstuffworks.com/historical-figures/first-lady1.htm

http://www.hoover.archives.gov/programs/firstladycaptions.pdf

http://www.pbs.org/wgbh/americanexperience/features/presidents-firstlady/

http://www.todayifoundout.com/index.php/2013/02/the-first-first-lady/

http://topics.blogs.nytimes.com/2008/07/14/first-ladies-a-short-history/?_r=0

http://www.whitehouse.gov/about/first-ladies

Martha Dandridge Custis WASHINGTON 1789–1797	Abigail Smith ADAMS 1797–1801	Martha Wayles Skelton JEFFERSON d. 1782	Dolley Payne Todd MADISON 1809–1817	Elizabeth Kortright MONROE 1817–1825	Louisa Catherine Johnson ADAMS 1825–1829	Rachel Donelson Robards JACKSON d. 1828	Hannah Hoes VAN BUREN d. 1819	Anna Tuthill Symmes HARRISON 1841

Harriet "Hal" Rebecca Lane (JOHNSTON) 1857–1861	Mary Anne Todd LINCOLN 1861–1865	Eliza McCardle JOHNSON 1865–1869	Julia Boggs Dent GRANT 1869–1877	Lucy Ware Webb HAYES 1877–1881	Lucretia "Crete" Rudolph GARFIELD 1881	Ellen "Nell" Lewis Herndon ARTHUR d. 1880	Frances Clara Folsom CLEVELAND (Preston) 1886–1889	Caroline Lavinia Scott HARRISON 1889–1892

Grace Anna Goodhue COOLIDGE 1923–1929	Lou Henry HOOVER 1929–1933	Anna Eleanor ROOSEVELT 1933–1945	Elizabeth "Bess" Virginia Wallace TRUMAN 1945–1953	Mamie Geneva Doud EISENHOWER 1953–1961	Jacqueline Lee Bouvier KENNEDY (Onassis) 1961–1963	Claudia Alta "Lady Bird" Taylor JOHNSON 1963–1969	Thelma Catherine "Pat" Ryan NIXON 1969–1974	Elizabeth "Betty" Ann Bloomer Warren FORD 1974–1977